Published by Creative Education and
Creative Paperbacks
P.O. Box 227, Mankato, Minnesota 56002
Creative Education and Creative Paperbacks
are imprints of The Creative Company
www.thecreativecompany.us

Design by The Design Lab
Production by Dana Cheit
Art direction by Rita Marshall
Printed in the United States of America

Photographs by Alamy (Rafael Ben-Ari, Tim Graham,
Yadid Levy, Navè Orgad, igor terekhov, Michel &
Gabrielle Therin-Weise, Vivid Africa Photography),
Dreamstime (Byvalet, Peng Ge, Isselee, Ying Feng
Johansson, Martyn Unsworth), iStockphoto (daboost,
DVrcan, Knaupe, pawopa3336)

Library of Congress Cataloging-in-Publication Data
Names: Bodden, Valerie, author.
Title: Llamas / Valerie Bodden.
Series: Amazing Animals.
Includes bibliographical references and index.
Summary: A basic exploration of the appearance,
behavior, and habitat of llamas, the long-necked
mammals native to South America's Andes
Mountains. Also included is a story from folklore
explaining how llamas came to be.
Identifiers: ISBN 978-1-64026-037-5 (hardcover)
/ ISBN 978-1-62832-625-3 (pbk) / ISBN 978-1-
64000-153-4 (eBook)

This title has been submitted for CIP processing under
LCCN 2018938938.

CCSS: RI.1.1, 2, 4, 5, 6, 7; RI.2.2, 5, 6, 7, 10;
RI.3.1, 5, 7, 8; RF.1.1, 3, 4; RF.2.3, 4

First Edition HC 9 8 7 6 5 4 3 2 1
First Edition PBK 9 8 7 6 5 4 3 2 1

LLAMAS

BY VALERIE BODDEN

CREATIVE EDUCATION • CREATIVE PAPERBACKS

Llamas still live in South America in places such as Peru

Llamas are mammals. They are related to camels. Llamas used to live in the wild in South America. But thousands of years ago, people tamed llamas.

mammals animals that have hair or fur and feed their babies with milk

tamed trained a wild animal to be kept by people

Llamas have long necks and small heads. They have big eyes and ears. Thick, woolly hair covers a llama. This coat can be black, white, gray, brown, or reddish. Some llamas are more than one color.

Llama ears are curved, or shaped like bananas

Llamas stand up to six feet (1.8 m) tall. That's as tall as some adult humans! The animals weigh 250 to 450 pounds (113–204 kg).

Friendly llamas can be trained easily

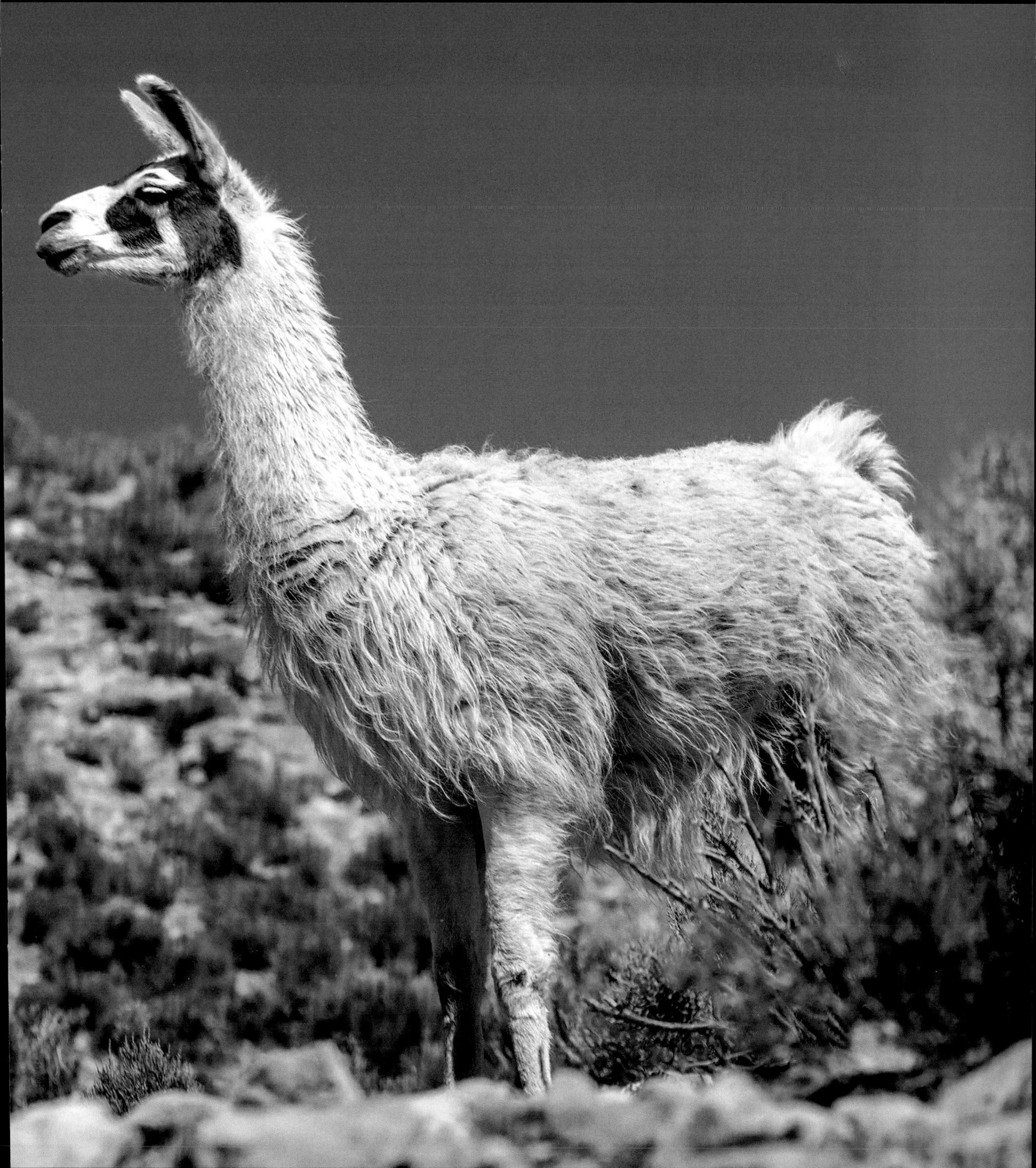

Wild llamas once lived in South America's high, cold Andes Mountains. Today, people still raise llamas in the Andes. People raise llamas in other parts of South and North America, too.

Llamas may be allowed to roam or kept in pens

Llamas eat grasses, shrubs, seeds, and fruits. On some farms, llamas are also fed grains and hay. A llama's top lip is split in the middle. Each side works like a finger to grab food. The lips push plants into the llama's mouth.

A llama's three-part stomach helps it eat tough plants

Crias can stand and walk within an hour of birth

A mother llama gives birth to one **cria** (*KREE-uh*) each year. The newborn weighs about 30 pounds (13.6 kg). The cria stays with its mother for six months. Most llamas live 20 to 30 years.

cria a baby llama

Llamas take care of one another, keeping each other safe

Llamas live in groups called herds. They spend a lot of time **grazing**. Some of the herd keeps watch for **predators** like wild dogs and foxes. If a predator attacks, adult llamas run toward it. They kick to drive it away.

grazing feeding on grasses growing on the land

predators animals that kill and eat other animals

Llamas talk to each other. They make a humming sound when they are happy. A high, loud call means they are scared. Males scream or grunt when they fight.

Male llamas may wrestle with their necks (above)

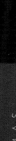

Some people keep llamas as pets. Others raise llamas for their woolly coats or to carry heavy loads. It can be fun to meet these gentle, friendly creatures!

People in Peru dress up their llamas for special events

A Llama Story

How did llamas come to be? The Inca told a story about this. A princess disobeyed her father, the king. So the king sent the princess and her husband to live in the mountains. But they were cold there. Their feet hurt from the rocks. So the Creator decided to help them. He changed them into animals with thick fur and tough feet. They became the first llamas.

Inca South American Indian peoples of the Andes Mountains

Read More

Aspen-Baxter, Linda, and Heather Kissock. *Llamas*. New York: AV2 by Weigl, 2012.

West, David. *Mountain Animals*. Mankato, Minn.: Black Rabbit Books, 2016.

Websites

Enchanted Learning: Llama
http://www.enchantedlearning.com/subjects/mammals/camel/Llamaprintout.shtml
This site has llama facts and a picture to color.

National Geographic Animals: Llama
http://www.nationalgeographic.com/animals/mammals/l/llama/
Learn more about llamas.

Note: Every effort has been made to ensure that the websites listed above are suitable for children, that they have educational value, and that they contain no inappropriate material. However, because of the nature of the Internet, it is impossible to guarantee that these sites will remain active indefinitely or that their contents will not be altered.

Index